Alphabet Zoo

written & illustrated
by
Adam J. Kudlack

Fomatting by Two Ton Productions, www.twotonproductions.com

Dedicated to my loving daughter Kayla.

A is for Alligator...

Alligators live near swamps and rivers. In the 1700's Spanish explorers sent word home

from South America of "terrible lizards"up to 20ft long, so many of them it was said that a

person could walk across their backs to get to the other side of a river.

Though there is no proof of anyone actually doing this, today this would be

impossible as there are just not enough alligators left. They were slaughtered in the

millions, mostly for their hides, until protected in the 1940's. Alligators seldom grow

larger than 13 feet but still can be dangerous man killers...

B is for Bear...

A polar bear! Polar bears live in the arctic regions of the world near the north pole. Polar

bears are great swimmers and have been seen in the open sea miles from land, swimming

at up to 4mph. On land they can run around 25mph. A polar bear's major source of food

is the ringed seal, a bear can pick up their scent from over a mile away... It is believed that

they can smell whale blubber from 20 miles away.

C is for Cougar...

Cougars are magnificent stealthy hunters, and have been known to attack humans, though

few have lived to tell the tale. Cougars were once widespread across the America's but

have been driven to inhospitable regions by man.

D is for Dolphin...

The playful dolphin has been appreciated by mankind for thousands of years. Ancient

roman coins depict young children riding on the backs of dolphins. The Greek

philosopher Plutarch wrote that the dolphin was the only creature to love man for his own

sake rather than for food. They use a highly-developed sonar system that can

distinguish different materials by the sound bouncing off of them.

E is for Elephant...

The elephant Ahmed the Great is depicted here on the eve of his death in the early 1970's.

Protected by an unique Presidential decree, he was guarded by game wardens 24 hours a day... He became a living symbol of Kenya's conservation of wildlife as he traversed the misty mountains of Marsabit. A likeness of his tusks and skin are on display in the National museum in Nairobi... His tusks recant days when Kenya was roamed by bulls with ivory weighing in more than 100 kilograms a pair...

F is for Frog...

A poison dart frog. Poison dart frogs are among the most poisonous of all the animal

kingdoms. Native tribes of South Americas rain forest know this and use the frogs poison

too coat their arrowheads to hunt with. One frog could coat up to fifty arrowheads.

Generally brightly colored either green, blue and black, sometimes with brownish gold or

yellow... They are much at home anywhere they go, for predators know their

markings and leave them alone. They have elaborate mating rituals and after the

eggs are laid in a small pool, the male watches over them. When they hatch, he carries

them on his back to a lake or stream...

G is for Gorilla...

The gorilla is the gentle giant in the jungle, normally a peaceful creature. When a threat is

present, a male will put up a show of strength by standing straight up, growling and

pounding his chest. If this doesn't work, he will sometimes charge only to swerve at the

last moment. Most families consist of between 5 and 15 and one dominant male known

as the silverback because of the graying hair on his back. The silverback leads his family

and protects them from dangers. Gorillas are intelligent problem solvers with excellent

memories, one in particular named Koko was taught sign language amd could

communicate using more than 1,000 different signs...

H is for Hippopotamus...

Hippos are normally calm, sometimes aggressive and generally inquisitive... In the late

1920's a hippo in South African Cape Region by the name of Hubert was known to

peep in doorways, trample yards, block roads and once even lying on a railroad track

stopping an oncoming train... It would be rare to have that happen now for the hippo

population has been reduced drastically. A graceful swimmer the hippo can also run faster

then a man, angry hippos are fearsome and with its huge teeth it is able to bite through

alligators...

I is for Impala...

The impalas scientific name Aepyceros means "high horn" in Greek, referring to the males

amazing lyre shaped horns... The impalas are prey for many predators, though its worst

enemy is the tick. The impala feeds in tick infested grasslands and the ticks drain lots of

blood... The impalas have that covered, its teeth have adapted to groom parasites from its

hide. The parts that can't be reached are groomed by another impala...

J is for Jay...

A Blue Jay! The bright azure blue is eye catching yet it has no blue pigment at all, rather

its feathers get their color through light refracting through them... Squash the feather and

the color disappears. When the blue jay spots an intruder in the forest it makes a raucous

Jay-Jay warning call... This popular bird has been depicted in books and cartoons and is

the sentinel of the woods and forests... Appearing elegant the blue jay blows its cover at

the feeder, shoving other birds out the way to feed... As an omnivore it performs a great

service by consuming the pupae of tent caterpillars, each pair feeding hundreds to their

nestlings in the early summer months.

K is for Koala...

Koalas are not bears yet marsupials. It has a tiny brain for its size, weighing in at about

0.2% of its total mass. This is thought to be an adaptation from its low energy diet of

eucalyptus leaves. Its diet is extremely specialized, eating only five out of the 350 species

of eucalyptuses. Bacteria in its stomach helps coping with the highly toxic leaves of which

it eats a pound a day. A hundred years ago the koala was almost wiped out by the fur trade

now protected since 1927. The koala has no sweat glands and cools itself by licking its

front legs and stretching out on a tree.

L is for Leopard...

A snow leopard... Few sights are as spectacular as a snow leopard traversing through the

mountains... It has huge paws and a tall hindquarters allowing it to jump 50ft horizontally

and 20ft vertically... Though they are on the endangered species list and protected these

majestic creatures are still hunted for their pelts. Other body parts and bones are used in

traditional Chinese medicine...

M is for Manatee...

A manatee can be found in the southern United States to the Caribbean islands and south to northeast Brazil. They can grow too almost thirteen feet long and weigh 3,300lbs... When a manatee first came into being around 5 to 14 million years ago, most plants they ate contained silica. This wore down their teeth so to fight this they adapted molars that would be continuously replaced. Old ones shed in the front and new ones growing from the rear. The manatee prefers to live in shallows, eating sea grass. Although protected this docile friendly sea cow is still hunted in some countries and boats pose a serious hazard. Their numbers are dropping, the most significant numbers being in southern Florida where habitat degradation and human pressure threaten extinction...

N is for Nightingale...

The nightingale's song is unique unlike any other bird song heard in Europe... As its name

suggests it does sing through the night and also during the day in shaded glens. Strangely

once the chicks hatch the singing stops and the nightingale calls harshly to it's young.

There are many tales of why the nightingale sings at night. Most tales say that they would

sing while having a thorn pressed against its breast in order to stay awake... It is said that

originally the nightingale only had one eye that it stole the single eye from a slow worm.

Ever since, the slow worm has been searching for the bird to get his eye back. So the

nightingale in fear of losing its eye sings all night to keep awake...

O is for Owl...

A snowy owl... The snowy owl's main diet is lemmings, when lemmings have a bad year

so do the owls. The lemming population affects how many owls reproduce and how many

young they will raise. Nesting owls need two lemmings a day and a family of owls could

eat as many as 1.500 lemmings before the young go off on their own. These days snowy

owls will take a variety of prey even preying on other raptors and when desperate will eat

fish or carrion. When food is short, the snowy owl can live off of fat reserves for six

weeks. They rarely seek shelter even from roaring winds and their plumage protects them

so well that adults can endure temps as low as 40'C or -40'F... This lovely owl is

protected throughout much of America and the UK yet in Alaska it is legal fore residents

to kill an unlimited number for food and clothing. A Romanian folklore tells of repentant

sinners flying to heaven as snowy owls

P is for Panda...

An ancient Chinese tale tells how a panda got its markings when a young girl, a friend of

the bears died. The pandas wept at the funeral and rubbed their arms over their eyes,

smudging them with black. Then they hugged one another for comfort and blackened

their ears, shoulders and rumps... A panda skin is worth $180,000 on the black market but

a Chinese poacher tempted to trade this endangered species will face the death penalty if

caught. Several poachers have been executed and China has shown further commitment to

protect this much loved bear. They have stopped logging within its range and have started

a national conservation program. Breeding these wonderful animals in captivity has not

been successful.

Q is for Quokka...

Quokka can be found on Rottnest Island and Bald Island off the coast of Australia. Dutch

explorers sailing around the coast of Australia passed a small island just six miles from

where the city of Perth is today... The island was infested with cat-sized rats so they gave

it the Dutch name rott nest, or rat's nest, island. The rats were actually quokkas. Today

more than 10,000 quokkas live on a predator free Rottnest with a few colonies spreading

around Perth... The young are suckled in the mother's pouch and once it suckling is over

its life depends on finding water and nitrogen content in food... During the day the males

fight furiously for the best shelter...

R is for Rhinoceros...

The white rhinoceros weighs in at up to 3 tons and has a flat lip that is flexible but not

hooked. The name white comes from the Afrikaans word weit, meaning wide and

referring to the lip. It feeds on grass rather than leaves. They are hunted for their horns

which are made into dagger handles or ground into powder to be used as medicine.

Though more numerous in numbers than its black counter part, the white rhino is still

protected and endangered. In an attempt to prevent poaching wardens have sedated rhinos

and removed their horns which aren't needed to survive. Yet poachers often kill hornless

animals to save themselves from having to track them again...

S is for Seal...

A weddell seal... Seals are stealthy hunters... They drift within a few feet of their prey and

snatch it quickly, mostly of which is cod. Weddell seals have acute vision and use the light

through the ice as backlighting to find prey... They have also been seen puffing small fish

out of icy cracks with puffs of air. Adult males can grow almost 10ft long and weigh in at

880lbs... The weddell seals inaccessibility protects them from hunting though many were

hunted to feed sled dogs...

T is for Tiger...

The tiger is not only awe inspiring yet also fearsome. A documented account of a man-eater in India was known to have killed 436 people. Today it is generally accepted that only old or injured tigers will attack humans rather than eat their normal prey. This mighty cats only predator is man. It has suffered drastically from being hunted as a trophy, for its beautiful skin and for many of its body parts which are used in traditional Chinese medicines. Three of the original eight subspecies are extinct and others are threatened. The Siberian tiger pictured here is most at risk... Only about 400 remain in the wild and despite heavy protection they are still being poached... Tigers striped patterns are unique like fingerprints no two are the same. Tigers are solitary rather than pack animals. The social group is generally the mother and her young who stay together for around 24-30 months until they are old enough to seek out there own territory... Tigers also hunt alone.

One bite from their incredible strong jaw is normally fatal...

U is for Urial...

The urial can be found in Western Central Asia... Its habitat consists of grassy slopes just

below the timberline. Urial's eat mostly grass but can eat leaves if need be... The urial's

existence is threatened as their habitat is perfectly suited for humans...

V is for Vulture...

The cape griffon vulture... One day in 1996 a careless farmer killed more than 200 of these

endangered birds with poison by mistake. Yet other farmers have poisoned these birds on

purpose fearing that they will spread disease through the cattle's drinking water. The cape

griffon is the second largest of the African vultures. It lives in the highlands and descends

to the grasslands to feed on carrion... The decline in hyenas has affected the vulture by

reducing the amount of bones that have been broken up into small fragments for calcium

needs. African witch doctors wear the skins of vultures a practice since outlawed in South

Africa and used in their traditional medicine. Also eating the brain of the vulture is

thought to bring clairvoyance and a dried cape griffon foot is thought to bring gamblers

luck...

W is for Wolf...

An arctic wolf... The arctic wolf spends fall and winter hunting in small packs or singly in

a constant quest for sustenance... In these months of darkness it can survive sub-freezing

temperatures and weeks without eating... Alone the wolf will hunt arctic hare and

lemmings. In a pack the wolves work together hunting larger prey like the caribou and

separate the young or weaker animals unable to outrun them. A caribou or musk ox would

feed a pack of wolves for almost a week. A smaller pack of arctic wolves is generally a

family group consisting of an alpha male and female, plus their offspring. The cubs are

born blind and feed from their mothers milk for the first four weeks and the pack

cooperates in feeding, regurgitating meat from the kill...

X is for Xantus...

The Xantus is a Mexican hummingbird found normally only in Baja California. Native

American people believe that the hummingbird is the symbol of the spreader of life on

earth. The average hummingbird's wings beat an amazing 53 times a second in normal

flight.

Y is for Yak...

For more than 3,000 years this tough sure footed, good natured creature has been domesticated by the people of Tibet. Not only does the yak serve as a work animal it also provides clothing and textiles from its wool like hair. The yak's rich low fat milk is made into butter and cheese. Dried yak dung is the only source of fuel for fires on the treeless Tibetan plateau. There are about 100,000 or so yaks in the wild and can cause a problem with domesticated animals. Wild males will rush herds and abduct females in heat, sometimes killing domesticated males. The numbers of this endangered species is threatened from illegal hunting.

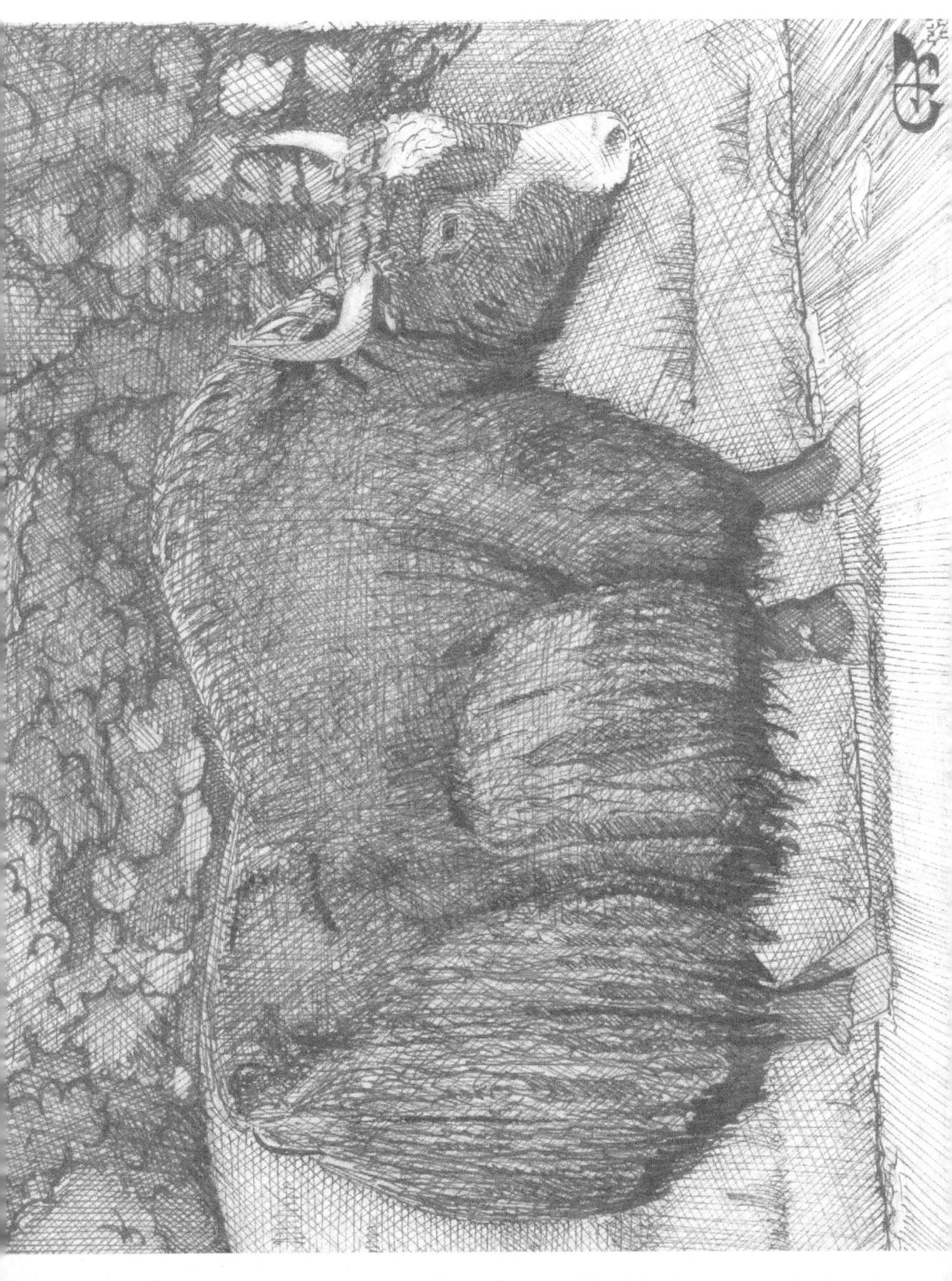

Z is for Zebra...

The purpose of the zebras stripes is unknown. Burchell's zebra depicted here is the only

one of the three zebra species actually not endangered... Making a constant migratory

circuit, circling clockwise 300 miles of the Serengeti and Masai Mara National Parks in

East Africa as the season so dictates. Plains zebras mix with herds of wildebeest for

protection and eat the grasses that they will not. They have been hunted for hides and

meat, but are now a mainstay for the tourist industry.

www.ingramcontent.com/pod-product-compliance
Lightning Source LLC
Chambersburg PA
CBHW081420280526
45788CB00009B/3170